THE COMPLETE GUIDE TO TENSION ADJUSTING

By

Alex Askaroff

To see Alex Askaroff's work
Visit Amazon
www.sewalot.com

The rights of Alex Askaroff as author of this work have been asserted by him in accordance with the Copyright, Designs and Patents Act 1993.
©

Introduction

Sewing machine thread tension adjustment falls into upper (top) and lower (bobbin case) adjustments. Therefore this booklet will also be in two sections, upper and lower.

> *This is a long and informative piece on tension. Put the kettle on and make yourself a nice cup of tea, then take your time to read it. It will be worth it in the end.*

For many people tension adjustment is an enigma inside a riddle. The mere thought of altering the tension makes some people shudder and run for the gin. Others move toward the machine, in fear, circling a few times, muttering to themselves, before attempting to touch anything.

I have known people throw sewing machines out of windows. I have seen women cry and men get mad over this one topic. Growing up in a factory full of sewing machines I soon came to learn many new words that I passed on to eager classmates at school, all because of the humble sewing machine.

I know someone—a man—who threw an industrial machine out of a third-floor window because of tension adjustment! Luckily I might add, no one was injured in the making of this booklet.

Well, the truth is that it is actually very easy to adjust your machine's tension so long as you follow simple procedures.

Before we start I must mention one point, although it is mainly women—over 90%—that sew, many men also sew; designers, upholsters, tailors, sail makers and so on. This adjustment pages works just as well for both sexes.

Too lose or too tight. What we are going to learn is how to get your machine 'Just Right'.

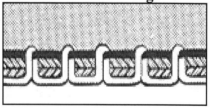

Let's get started

TOP TENSION ADJUSTMENT

Start by looking at the machine.

As you sit at the machine most of them have a tension regulator directly facing the user. A numbered dial that may go from 1-9 or 1-4 or, on older machines, it may simply be a knob that turns. On some older machines the tension regulator is on the end of the machine, sometimes on top.

All tension regulators work on the same principle. The upper thread passes between spring-loaded discs. By turning the dial clockwise or anticlockwise you increase or decrease the pressure on the thread as it passes through.

Do not be afraid to turn your tension dial. A skilled operator may alter the tension many times while sewing a garment that varies in thickness.

Go try turning your dial.

> **First though, note where it is before you start and make sure you put it back to that mark.**

Now did that feel good? Once you get used to adjusting your tension you will be able to impress friends and influence people. Well, not quite, but you will have the satisfaction of being the most popular person in your quilting class!

One important note. There are many machines on the market today that say 'AUTOMATIC' Tension. Is there really such a thing? I doubt it. Is there a little Pixie sitting inside your machine waiting for your fabric? Does he peek out of a small hole in the top of your machine? "Ah top of the morning to you, that material is thin but I reckon dense, so I'll put your tension just there!"

In reality most of these machines use the same old dials with the numbers removed and AUTOMATIC written on them. I know, I used to sell them.

There are a few complex computer machines that also boast automatic tension, but they still can have trouble. It is a great selling point but you do need to learn to adjust your tension if you have a tension dial.

HOWEVER, there are those few computer machines that really do have self-adjusting mechanisms, but we are not concerned with them as they really do adjust the tension for you. They use a combination of motors and sensors to work out how thick your work is (by the height of the presser foot) and the pressure on the work. Then a little sensor adjust the tension internally. Surprisingly, though they cost a small fortune, they are not always the best machines for a perfect stitch. Let us look at normal sewing machines.

As you turn your tension dial clockwise, you are increasing the tension. Anticlockwise, decreasing it.

The lighter the pressure on the dial the lighter the upper tension is in the fabric. What we are looking for, in a perfect stitch, is one that is interlocked evenly in the middle of the fabric layer.

> For an illustration, open your hands and face them toward each other with your fingers apart. Now slide them together, interlocking your fingers as if in prayer. If you look at the palms of your cupped, joined, hands you will see the formation of a perfect interlocked stitch. This is what we are trying to get on your sewing machine. If the stitch is unbalanced the top or bottom thread can be easily pulled out. This gives you a weak stitch.

There are the usual classic faults in tension. Loose threads, looping, puckering, bunching and many more. What we want to do is eliminate them all by understanding the simple procedure of tension adjustment. I have listed in my Sewing Machine Fault Finding Booklet, on Amazon, the other faults that can affect your sewing machine and that are not covered by tension adjustment.

OK, so here goes. We know that a simple twist of the wrist on the tension dial can be the difference between a perfect stitch and one that drives you crazy.

Firstly we must make sure the tension unit is working. Whatever number your tension dial goes up to, place it at half that, so you are in the middle of the dial. If your dial is un-numbered, turn from lowest to highest tension and judge the halfway point, set the adjustment to that point.

Put a reel of thread on your machine and thread the monster. Finally pull the thread through the needle's eye with the foot raised.

> The reason the foot must be raised is that MOST machines have an automatic tension-disc release connected to the presser foot. As you raise the foot the discs release, allowing you to pull the thread through without bending the needle too much or breaking the thread.

Check that this is working. Pull the thread through with the foot up, then lower the foot and see what happens when you pull the thread with the foot down. It should become tight to pull.

If the thread is not tight enough to bend the needle—

- your tension dial is not working properly, or
- the tension so low that it does not work, or
- the thread is not in the tension unit properly

At this point we must stop and talk about threads.

Some old threads cause so much trouble that they are better thrown away. Some threads are lumpy, some perish and some threads are riddled with knots.

When adjusting your machine always use a good quality thread. I, myself, prefer polyester threads as they give a good quality stitch with a bit of give. Not many people realise that the top thread passes through the eye of the needle many times before it finally gets taken up in the fabric. You can see this, for yourself, by marking the thread above the needle and watching it as you turn the machine by hand. Polyester threads bear up to this rubbing—through the eye of the needle—much better than cotton. But, whatever threads you use, make sure it is of good quality.

You can carry out a little test here. Pull an arm's length of thread off the reel and hold it between your hands so that the thread drops in front of you in a wide U shape. Move your hands closer together and see what the thread does. If you have a balanced thread nothing will happen. If you have an unbalanced thread the thread, as it gets closer together, suddenly twists around itself. This causes lots of problems, twisting around thread guides and jamming into tension disks. Do not use unbalanced thread.

In normal sewing, never mix threads on a machine unless you want to visit the lunatic asylum.

> If the tension disks appear to be too loose, even on the tightest (clockwise) setting, and the thread is not being gripped, first check that the thread is between the disks, then check that there is nothing jammed between the disks that stops them from squeezing the thread (gently pry them apart, with minimum tension and look). You may have to dig out any remnants of thread that has become wound around the middle stud.
>
> If the tension disks appear to be too tight, on the loosest setting,

> the disks may be rusty or there may be a foreign object lodged between them. Remove any foreign material. You might be able to polish lightly rusted disks by using light string around the disk slot and pulling it back and forth. In severe cases consult your repair person.

Back to business. Now that we have made sure the tension unit is working we need to adjust it to get a lovely stitch in your work. What we must do at this point is find an average balance for the average material. So get some normal fabric, say a strip of clothing-weight cotton cloth. Fold it double as if you were going to sew a seam. Place it under the machine and start to sew. Now examine the stitch. Remember what we are looking for—a balanced, even, stitch on the top and bottom, with the lock right in the middle of both layers.

> A quick test you can carry out at this point is to get the end of one of the threads that is coming from the stitched material and pull it sharply. If it snaps on the first couple of stitches then it means the stitch is securely in the fabric. However if the thread can be pulled out you will need to adjust your machine tension.

One point to note is that you can have a secure stitch that is too tight and puckers the work. We will deal with that shortly.

IMPORTANT At this point I must bring to your attention a really important factor. The top tension controls the quality of the **underneath** stitch in your fabric. It is the top thread that is being taken, by your machine, around the lower thread and then pulled back up. Too little top tension will not bring the lower thread far enough, too much will pull the lower thread right through both the fabric layers.

If you are still with me then things are looking good, have your eyes started to glaze over yet? Be patient we are on our way. Think of it as searching for the Holy Grail of tension balancing. At the end of your journey you will be enlightened and your path through the maze of tension adjusting will be clear.

Back to business again. What we need to do now is to alter the stitch according to what the problem is. The lower section of the page deals with lower tension adjustment. I must impress on you that you should carry out Upper Tension Adjustment first, as this is much easier and the most common cause of a poor stitch, 9 times out of 10 in fact.

If you have a perfect **underneath** stitch but a straight-line stitch on top and turning the tension dial has no effect, go to lower thread adjustment, further down the page.

> **Note** Some of the large reels of thread available today can alter a well-balanced machine and throw the stitch balance out because they are harder to turn when the tread is unwinding. If you are having tension trouble and are using a large reel of thread, wind the thread onto a bobbin and place the bobbin on top of the machine and use it like a small reel of thread. Now continue.

What is the problem with your stitch? Is it all *loopy* underneath? This is the most common problem.

> If you have a big mess underneath then your **top** tension is not functioning or you have threaded the machine wrongly. See my Sewing Machine Fault Finding Booklet on Amazon.

So, here we are at last, down to the nitty-gritty. It is so simple that it hurts. By adjusting the top tension clockwise the loops will slowly disappear. Run along about 6 inches of fabric and examine the underneath stitch. Alter the numbers one at a time, say from 4 to 5, check each time you do. Keep going until you find that the top and bottom match. Remember the hands? Now, the number that you have reached on your dial is the **BALANCE POINT**.

It does not matter what the number is. All machines, like humans, are slightly different. One machine may run beautifully on number 2 while another machine of the same type will be running on number 7.

A professional sewing machine engineer usually balances your tension dial internally to the middle so that you may increase or decrease it. This is an internal adjustment for 'trained' experts.

Once you have found this **BALANCE POINT** make sure you remember it. From this number you should be able to sew 90% of all fabrics. You may decrease the number for lighter work, say nets or satin, and increase it for curtains or denim. But always put the tension back to this point.

If the top and bottom tensions are balanced but both too tight the fabric will pucker. Loosen both top and bottom tensions a little at a time (lower thread adjustments) until a smooth stitch is created.

To finish off the top tension adjustment, one final point. It will not matter how many times you adjust your tension dial; master the dial and the world will be yours. Well done.

LOWER THREAD TENSION ADJUSTMENT

ONLY FOR THE BRAVE

In many instruction manuals it will say something like: **the lower tension is set at the factory and should not be adjusted.**

That is all well and good but twenty years have passed, the factory closed and your tensions are all over the place. You have sewing to do and you want it right!

One of my masters took me, at the tender age of seventeen, through the basics of tension adjustments, then spent the next twenty years trying to hammer it into me how important correct tension is to every sewing machine ever made, no matter whether it is the latest all-singing all-dancing computer, that talks to you and does the washing up for you, or a hundred-year-old antique that simply looks lovingly at you but won't perform.

If you are having trouble with your sewing machine stitch quality and you have done all the usual things, like playing around with the top tension for a week, thrown the machine out of the bedroom window and then tried to see if it will still work before telling your partner that you were burgled and the thieves dropped your machine whilst escaping. There is the possibility that the lower tension of the machine is out of balance. Now before we go any further, do not, I repeat, **do not** adjust your machine if you are happy with your stitch.

A simple test if your tensions are well balanced is to sew a piece of cotton fabric about six inches in length then get the ends of the thread that are left and give them a sharp tug. If the tensions are good the thread should snap without pulling out of the work. In other words you have a proper LOCK STITCH. If you find that the thread is pulling out of one side or the other then the stitch is out of balance and your threads are not locked into the fabric leading to a weak seam.

Tension balancing is a little understood procedure and many so-called repair people will mess around with the wrong part of your machine and make little or no improvement. How many of you have taken your sickly machines into a shop for a service and received them back smothered in oil and not much better—with a nice bill for nothing.

Well, here goes. I will try and explain the enigma that has eluded people for so long. Even the great inventor Isaac Singer had terrible trouble getting the tensions right on his first patent model, so you are not alone.

The classic symptoms of lower tension collapse are quite obvious. Look at your stitch and see if the lower thread has pulled through to the top of the fabric. The underneath will look fine, perhaps a little loose—however, the top thread will be able to be pulled out of the fabric. This is because the loop in the lower thread is laying on top of the fabric, not pulling the top thread into the fabric.

You will notice, with this symptom, that you have little or no effect by altering the top tension dial and often think that it is a top tension dial fault. That is wrong.

OK, so here goes, hold on tight, it is going to get nasty, have your painkillers ready.

Step one, setting the top tension. Assuming that your top tension is working can be a fatal flaw but is easily checked. Most sewing machines, even quite early ones, have automatic top tension release mechanisms. This means that, once the sewing foot is raised, the top thread tension is automatically released so that you can pull your work out of the machine without the thread breaking. To test this simply raise the sewing foot, set the needle to its highest position and see if the thread pulls out easier than if the foot was lowered ready for sewing.

To **test** if the thread is being held properly by the tension discs, when ready for sewing, you need to lower the foot then grasp the thread where it comes out of the eye of the needle and pull. The thread **on all machines** should be tight enough to bend the needle when pulled.

If it does not then you need to investigate why it is not tight. The most common reason is a restriction, between the tension discs themselves, caused by fluff, or corrosion or trapped threads. A loose top thread leads to a bunching of thread **underneath** the work (or looping, with minor tension failure).

Once you have done the test, put your numbered tension dial halfway. For instance if you have a dial that goes from one to four put it on two, one to nine put in between the four and five. Get the idea? On older machines with no tension-dial numbers turn the dial clockwise until the thread bends the needle when pulled through as I have just mentioned.

Then leave the top thread tension alone.

> Well, by now only the mad will still be with me, the brave and the foolish have left for pizza and we have not even got to the lower thread tension that we are going to discuss.

Now the lower tensions fall into basically two types for lockstitch machines. Ones with bobbin cases and ones without. We have to deal with each separately but both have common symptoms and cures so I will take the machines with bobbin cases first.

It is important to say, at this stage, that sewing threads alter a great deal in thickness and 'stickyness'. I once had a call out to Brighton District General Hospital because twelve machines had all broken down on the same day, only to discover it was a faulty batch of new thread.

If you look closely at, for instance, a new polyester and put it against an old reel of cotton (you know the one that you just could not throw away from your granny's old stuff because you might just need a sunset-orange thread one day) you will notice that the new polyester thread can be up to half the thickness of the old cotton one.

In simple terms this means that by switching from polyester to the old cotton you have instantly changed the thread tension by a huge amount and this can lead, instantly, to a poor stitch. How many times have you put your trusty old sewing machine away, working perfectly, and a few days later it is messing about? What you have not realised is that it is possible that the change in thread has caused this problem. Some sticky, old, cottons are only fit for hand sewing or tacking or winding onto your husband's fishing reel so that he can tell you of the monster that got away.

Always keep a reel of new, white, polyester thread handy and, if your machine plays up, switch to it and see if the stitch is better. Nine times out of ten the thread is the culprit and you just have to be brave and bin it. Or chuck it at a neighbour's cat that has just dug up your flower bed—perfect weight and size for that, so I am told.

Now where was I? Oh yes, back to the all-important bobbin-case thread adjustment.

Wind a full bobbin of new white thread, the same type that you normally sew with—it is not important if it is silk, cotton, polyester or a mix—just your usual thread. Place the bobbin into the bobbin case and suspend the bobbin by the thread, like a spider hanging from its web. If, when you hold the thread, the case simply drops to the floor you need to adjust the bobbin-case screw clockwise until it just holds its own weight.

It is not so important which way you put the bobbin into the case. Some find a machine sews better with the bobbin going one way, some the

> other, only trial and error points this
> out for your machine. Loads of
> people are going to disagree with
> this, never mind.

Now, while the spider, oops, bobbin and case are suspended by the thread simply jerk your hand a little and see what the case does.

> Now we are getting to the nitty-gritty
> of tension adjustment the real bread
> and beans of the matter.

So, when you shake it a little the bobbin case drops a little. This is the MAGIC point, known in the trade as the balance point, for your type of thread. If the case does not move you need to adjust the bobbin-case screw anticlockwise until it drops a little when lightly jerked. Only turn the screw a small part of a turn each time, then dangle-check again. Once you have mastered this adjustment you will be in great demand at all sewing classes as you transform misbehaving sewing machines in an instant.

> Hold on, I am not finished, no happy
> dancing just yet, no running out and
> buying twenty lottery tickets because
> you feel lucky (remember me if you
> win).

Although this is the balance point some machines need to be adjusted slightly tighter or looser for the perfect stitch. When adjusting from this point make only very small movements of the screw, about one sixteenth of a turn at a time. After each adjustment run a trial stitch and examine. Once you are right with the lower tension you can go back to the top tension unit again and make final adjustments, say from a four to a five, or a four to a three, to get it just perfect.

Adjusting the newer type plastic cases that are set permanently into the machine, you know, the ones where you just drop in the bobbin and hook it around the spring plate, is much the same. You need to do this more by feel. You need to FEEL the thread resistance by pulling the thread. One of the ways to do this is to place a fine hand-sewing needle partway into a cork—*Pinch one of your husband's or better still open up a new bottle of wine with dinner!*—so that about two inches (50 mm) of the needle is protruding from the cork. Then tie the thread from the machine case through the eye of the needle and, while holding the bottom of the cork, pull the thread. It should have a slight resistance and slightly, only slightly, bend the needle.

If it does not bend the needle you need to tighten the case-adjustment screw clockwise. If it bends too much you need to loosen it a little. Remember, tiny adjustments only. Well, hey presto! That is it.

If you can master lower thread adjustment you will have a control of your machine, actually ALL MACHINES rather than them controlling you!

One final point—by now the painkillers for that pounding headache have started to work—if you mix your threads it is a lottery whether the tensions will work effectively. **The worst culprits** are the old wooden reels of cotton that can become hard, springy, weak and sticky. They can really mess up your sewing machine—big time. Try and stick to the same upper and lower threads. If in doubt about a thread bin it! Really, all the grey hairs and profanities it can cause are just not worth it.

In my opinion, after a lifetime in the sewing trade, no thread performs better than a quality spun polyester, whatever fabric you are sewing.

I hope this has helped many of you that have a tension problem. Now you know why instruction books hardly ever mention lower thread adjustments.

Elvis has left the building.

THE COMPLETE GUIDE TO TENSION ADJUSTING ©

By Alex Askaroff

Want information on how to repair and adjust a sewing machine?

See my Sewing Machine Fault Finding Booklet on Amazon.

Most of us know the name Singer but few are aware of his amazing life story, his rags to riches journey from a little runaway to one of the richest men of his age. The story of Isaac Merritt Singer will blow your mind, his wives and lovers his castles and palaces all built on the back of one of the greatest inventions of the 19th century. For the first time the most complete story of a forgotten giant is brought to you by Alex Askaroff.

*If this isn't the perfect book it's close to it!
I'm on my third run though already.
Love it, love it, love it.
F. Watson USA*

Printed in Great Britain
by Amazon